PERMISSION TO Speak

PERMISSION TO Speak

ANN CHATHAM

Permission to Speak

Copyright © 2019 by Ann Chatham. All rights reserved.

No part of this publication may be reproduced, stored in a retrieval system or transmitted in any way by any means, electronic, mechanical, photocopy, recording or otherwise without the prior permission of the author except as provided by USA copyright law.

These poems are a work of fiction. Names, descriptions, entities, and incidents included in the story are products of the author's imagination. Any resemblance to actual persons, events, and entities is entirely coincidental.

The opinions expressed by the author are not necessarily those of URLink Print and Media.

1603 Capitol Ave., Suite 310 Cheyenne, Wyoming USA 82001
1-888-980-6523 | admin@urlinkpublishing.com

URLink Print and Media is committed to excellence in the publishing industry.

Book design copyright © 2018 by URLink Print and Media. All rights reserved.

Published in the United States of America

ISBN 978-1-64367-785-9 (Paperback)
ISBN 978-1-64367-784-2 (Digital)

05.08.19

Contents

An Empty Billy Can 9
Allah's Mercy 11
Australia's Child 12
I Wanna Know what Love Is 13
O Colin! 15
Crucifying Truth 16
Damaged 17
The farewell Song 18
Gratitude for What has Passed 20
Journey 22
Looking For Troy 23
Ode To The Murrumbidgee 24
Poison 26
Reflections At The Walking Track 27
Roy 28
Travelling Through Time 29
The Bell 31
The castle 33
The Stone 34
Three sons Of A Dead Man 35
Tomorrow's Crim 36
Shrew The Younger 38
The death Of Nanna 39
The Fabric 40
Be Gone 42
Assaulted Housewife 44
The Rock Orchid 45
Wollongong 46
The Harvest 48
The Answer 50
Hope 52

The lament of the constipated Dog 54
Daddy Long Legs 56
In A Flash 58
Monster 60
Sack him! 62
Storm At Sea 63
There Is Still Time 64
Waiting for the train 66
When The Bottle Is Empty 68
The Zippi-Uppi-Thing 69
For The Love Of Little Things 70
Let's Be Honest 72
Questions 74
The Spider 75
The Author 76

The poems between the covers of this book tell the story of compassion and the search for justice. They record relationships between people and how they use their giftedness for both good and evil (often in the same individual) Some poems, such as 'Colin' and 'Troy' are light hearted and funny where people are discovered in awkward situations and have been the subject of a story told in verse.

Many of my poems have a spiritual insight; a conversation with God, if you will that has troubled my sleep until I write it down.

I hope you find, in 'Permission To Speak' a vision of the great and the small; of the blameless and the guilty that makes life's story rich in its complexity.

An Empty Billy Can

"Take this empty billy can to uncle Alby's place
His nectarine tree is full of fruit
And they will go to waste.
He asked that you – his favourite niece
Would be the only one
To help him gather up the fruit
And he would give us some."
Alby was an ugly man
His face was tiny bubbles.
Unaware when I arrived.
That he began my troubles.

He took me in and lied me down
And licked his lips with glee.
His tongue hung out his drooling mouth
With what he'd done with me.

She cooked the fruit that I took home.
She made it into jam.
A week had passed – I went again
For Alby's evil plan.
Obedient child that I must be.
A prostitute at only three
With an empty billy can.

Where can I go?
I can't go back.
If I tell mum I'll get a smack

But Nanna says that God is near
And he will show me not to fear.
Nanna says God's here with me
No matter where that "here" would be.

So God and I became as one
He stayed from then when I was young.
We grew together; he and me.
The prostitute at only three.

Allah's Mercy

How dare you kill another man
How dare you take God's place.
What will you say to Allah
When you meet him face -to face?

Will you point to God his many sins
With need to take him down.
Or will you boast that you are king
With rights to wear the crown?

Don't ask for mercy then of God
You killers blind with hate.
The angels with their flaming swards
Are waiting at the gate.

The spirit of our martyrs
Will stand at Allah's side
And direct his angels to the place
Where hatred cannot hide.

Stay away from there Australia
For to Hell it will descend.
Find countries made of better stuff.
Where mercy is a friend.

Australia's Child

Cradled in a wooden box
In a hut with dirt for floor
Her mother barely sixteen years of age.
Frightened. Unprotected was
Australian born and bred.
Barely clean and often times unfed.
The first child of the family
Who opened up the page
Fled away to Europe
To escape the poorpar's cage.
Her father, He's a drunkard
All their money went on grog
Or spent on women in the pub at night.
He would share with them the stories
Of his children home in bed
And the wife who didn't love him
He's Australian born and bred.
The male child, he was different
He wouldn't go to school
Then he grew on into manhood unprepared.
He looked up to his father
And all the fun he had.
So he grew to be just like him.
Pot bellied, drunk and loud.
The wogs – he didn't like them
They worked too hard for him
And they didn't speak his language after all.
He could shoot them all he told us.
"They don't belong" he said.
They cannot be just like us
We're Australian born and bred.

I Wanna Know What Love Is

As I laid my heads on my pillows that night
My eyes in the darkness saw Clive.
The life that had left the man in the box
came to tell me that love was his drive.

A song came to mind
From a Foreigner's line
That answered my prayer
From a placeless somewhere.
With the face of the man in the box.

"I Wanna Know What Love Is"
There his grieving world stood
'Round the casket of wood.
Searching and tearful and empty.

"I want you to show me."

In a moment that fleeted
Their presence was greeted
By the memories of all that he stood for.
That of a father, of husband, of friend.
And much more.

"I wanna feel what Love is"

The justice. The laughter. The wisdom of years
His sorrow. His anger his weakness and fears.

"I know you can show me."

What did he give us
This man from the box?
A love and a life that is Clive.

O Colin!

I heard a little gossip
From the fairy at our table
That he saw Colin smiling
In the hallway before dawn.
He had tiptoed out a bedroom
Left three women sleeping there.
The look he wore suggested
That he didn't give a care!
'Round the table- at the telling
There were gasps of disbelief.
"Colin! O dear Colin.
The women's virtue -
What a thief!
He joined us late for breakfast,
Smiling widely.
Unaware.
That his adventure was uncovered
By the fairy on the stair.

Crucifying Truth

Julian it's Easter time and crucifixion looms.
Norway has its silver coin,
America your tomb.
Exposing lies for all to see -
A Christ-like thing to do,
Corruption has no hiding place;
And they're coming after you.
In secrecy your judges meet
Outraged by what you did.
Make ready the crown of thorns brave soul
Of truth they must be rid.

Damaged

Damaged my sense of humor.
Crushed and beaten-
Badly bruised.
I think somebody hurt it
Till it no longer was amused.

With my sense of humor ailing
I am not myself at all;
Without it I am helpless. –
It will lead to my downfall.

It used to thrive on belly laughs.
With a tiny touch of crude.
Now in an empty, hostile place
Sickly, sensibly conclude-

That poverty of humor
Is a poverty of mirth
That my place without a giggle
Is a place devoid of worth.

So I'm praying for a healer
Who will say "Just let it rest."
The problem isn't terminal
It just needs to convalesce.

The farewell Song

There are some people leaving us
But said we shouldn't make a fuss.
Ya Know – we think we will.
Cause they've been so very good to us.
Taught us heaps and cared for us.
Patched our scratches, rang our mums
And in the classroom taught us sums.

Two very different ladies they—
One in the office had to stay
We hear her on the phone to say
"There's nothing wrong. It's only Kay.
But Fred got hurt today at play
And needs for you to come.

Don't hurry though
He may not go
Improvement - He's begun to show
'cause soccer's on the field you know.

The other – from the classroom come.
A gentle soul. -A prayerful one.
A teacher of respect has won.
Loved by all – and feared by some.

The dogs -they are her special friend.
The lives of some on her depend
She saved them from a sticky end
and gave them peace of mind.

She sees that God is in us all
The short, The brave, The scared, The tall.

And will be sorely missed.

So off you go. You women two
But as you do know we all love you.

Gratitude for What has Passed

I have a bag of gratitude I want to share with you.
Of sadness, joy and wondering.
Of friendships tried and true.

I'm grateful for the places
Where learning has begun
In rooms, on fields and buses
And places filled with fun.

I'm grateful too; to those of you
Who worked me harder than I would
From you I've learned to persevere
And be more than I could.

I'm grateful for the differences
In the friends I have that's true.
For those who simply listen
And those who move and do.

For friends so loud with laughter
Who fill the room with joy
To those who quietly touched me
With wisdom to employ.

I'm grateful for the failures
That I'd suffered until now
They have taught me a great lesson;
- Life changes every hour.

I'm grateful for the people
Whom I was guided by;
Rule makers and comfort shakers
Have told me "harder try!".

I'm grateful for the open hearts
Of every one of you;
I'll cherish as I move along
To places old and new.

I'm grateful for the creatures too
In God's created day
All those who walk and fly and crawl
Incline my heart to pray.

Look back upon the year that was
With gratitude and grace;-
For somewhere in its hidden debts
The Christ child showed his face.

Journey

I have it come and talk.
Take my hand and we will walk
Through the inner self of thee.
First we'll enter into darkness,
Lighting corners of despair
Just to clear away the lies that linger there.
And then we'll cross the desert
Left by hot unthinking tongues
Where seldom falls a drop of rain
Of love for anyone.
Then If you're still with me
On this road to inner self
We have the last great danger spot:
The swamp of selfishness.
This place will surely drown you
Many travellers lose their way.
While clutching after gold and wealth
Not thinking price to pay
But we find that gold's too heavy
It will drag the spirit down
We often find them suffering
In the swampy underground.
Step softly through the danger spots
And always carry light.
So don't be fooled by passers by
Who offer gold at night.

Looking For Troy

This day we met at Shellharbour beach to stroll the shore along.
And to meet a fellow we hadn't met who wanted to come along.
Col told him where to meet us – What we looked like – What he'd see.
We would meet him in the car park just beyond the shady tree.

Col assured us, when we gathered, that Troy would meet us
Where he said.
We waited past the hour, then without him walked ahead.
To prove how kind the group could be
A friend and I went back to see -
If he turned up late where he was meant to be.

We had never met this person, so we didn't have a clue
Of just what we were looking for. The only thing we knew –
Was that he was over fifty, alone and looking lost.
So we asked each likely fellow, "Are you alone and are you lost?"

One man we followed to the pool had his lunch in a plastic bag.
We stopped and asked the question. He was really quite a wag.
He said he could be Troy for us – if we really wanted one.
He said he could be anything that turned out to be fun.

So we discovered; my friend and me
That no Troys swam in Shellharbour sea.
There were no Troys who lapped the pool.
Or walked on the beach; or sat on a stool.
No Troys stood by the toilet door.

There were no Troys at all we saw.
So we called his name up and down the shore.
Till our companions came and we called no more.

Ode To The Murrumbidgee

Camping in the bush this year
Was quite a lot of fun.
Though facilities are Spartan
Down where the rivers run.
Take in point the toilet block;
One long – drop in a shed.
The smell 'round noon is awful.
A visit then I dread.
So I had to time my toilet stops
For the deed to suit my need.
Not too early after daylight
For the seat is cold indeed.
The tin shed freezes overnight
The can inside – an unwelcome plight.
My comfort to impede.
I also have to make my run
Before the blowflies know I've come.
Before the sun warms up their wings.
Before they join me in my doings.

Why do I go?
I hear you say,
With the civilised so far away.
To stand at midnight among the stars.
Unpolluted by your smoke and cars.
To delight in a choir that welcomes the day
Made of song birds and the dance they play.
The mopoke was first to rise.

To break the darkness still
Followed by jackass wise,
His laughter loud and trill
Next the magpie's carolling sweet.
While chattering parrots kept the beat.
Just when I thought my day fulfilled
Came the ballet of swallows
Their vision thrilled.
These tiny birds danced their tale for me
In and around their nesting tree.
Together they all flew as one
To gather insects to feed their young.

What need have I of civilise;
Of clocks, of phones, of compromise?
When the wilderness has offered me
Some time to be completely free.

Poison

Mixed in a cauldron of smallness and fear
Served to the shallow and thirsty my dear.
'Tis stuff that will cripple the wounded and kill
What's left of a family,
For the chemist's sad thrill.

Thirst can be quenched by a serving of truth
To the father who loved,
By the sons of his youth.

Don't swallow corruption.
But pity the cook.
Love the vessel of smallest;
Her fear overlook
The spite caused disruption.
By an empty heart took.

Reflections At The Walking Track

Ten of us met at the walking track to get some exercise To wander through the park land and reduce our body size.
We gathered at the rock wall just inside the gate
And waited for some stragglers – who were sorry they were late.

All present and accounted for we started down the hill.
Some people striding off in front while others strode at will.

As we walked along we talked along
About things we knew and didn't.
It struck me about this group we share
And the people who are in it.

Some like to eat at restaurants, play cards and dance around.
Some paddle on the water. Some peddle on the ground.

Some meet and marry others or form friendships made for life.
While others just want things to do in a place devoid of strife.

There is one thing we all agree – no matter what we do.
This group is most important to provide for me and you.
- a place to go in company reliable and true.

Roy

They said they smelled him coming
As he staggered down the street,
And when he fell they only stopped to laugh.
For you couldn't help a drunkard,
He's not worth the time it took
Simply to bend and lift him
Or his face out of the dirt.
He stretched out a bony trembling hand To all the passers by.
But his fingernails were dirty
And we are just too shy.
His army coat was tattered
And he dribbled when he spoke
Which made a mud – pool 'round his face
No sight for gentle folk.

It takes one who has known suffering
To comfort those in pain
It takes on who knows that he is poor.
To give to one the same.
Mother! Where are you gentle one?
I need your comforting.
I need your hand out of this dirt
So I may go again.

Travelling Through Time

My dearest friend is dying.
She phoned me yesterday
to say that she is frightened
and I don't know what to say.

I will go to her tomorrow.
For a time with her I'll stay.
We will share our lasting friendship
In this life with which we play.

We'll remember in this place we share
Our travelling through time
The fun we had, the games we played.
That made our spirits shine.

In our friendship shared together.
At times we were inclined
to drink too much
and laugh too loud
At lovers hers and mine.

At times invading sadness
threatened tearing peace apart.
I'll remind her, when I visit.
Of our true collective heart.

We might listen to some music.
For my friend, she has a gift
of creating sweetest melodies
to give this world a lift.

I'll try my hardest not to pray
And ask the God to let her stay.
I know the answer.
God will say
That all that lives must go that way.

The Bell

While sorting through the things I had
Not needed any more
I came across my bell and saw -
It's memories fond and blessed.
For forty years and more it sat
Upon the teacher's desk.
It waited to be called upon
To bring the class to rest.
Calling for a change of task
To herald an address.

This bell; it sat as sentinel
And watched without a word
But held within it's metal hart
The classrooms seen and heard.

I placed the bell in front of me
And probed it for its memory
In fleeting moments I could see
Our vision of the past.

Forty years from young to old.
Forty years of children told
Forty years of friendships made
In forty years the games we've played

Some blessings that the bell could share
Of struggling children needing care.

Those bright and cheeky lively ones
Whose future in their eyes had shone
Their light upon the world to come.

Oh bell, you call me, "look behind"
For people who were true and kind.
But sadly bell you bring to mind
Some power hungry cruel and blind.

Of all the things I throw this day
I will not cast my bell away
For in its hollow underside
Are memories held
Not cast aside.

The castle

Enthroned there in your castle by the sea
Demanding that all should come
And pay to thee a homage.
To do thy bid - to reverence thee.
But they of freedom come for just a while And drift away.
Beyond the widening wilderness they stray.
Not prepared are they to feed to thee
What thou doest hunger for.
The power to rule beyond thy castle draw.
The kinsmen retreat away
From the shadows of thy realm.
Leaving only those who do thy bidding stay.
But stay he alone before thy lofty throne.
Only the jester stands, wringing hat in hands
Ready to dance at your majesty's command.

The Stone

How strange the world about us is today.
The people on the city streets like stones.
No expressions of humor in their voices.
No signs of sadness in their faces -
And still the fire burns.

Towering buildings like monsters
Peering down upon the moving multitude
Through tinted pains of glass
But cannot see
As people do not see or hear
Nor even feel the wanting needs of hunger-And still the fire burns.
His pay rise does not come -
The stone man cries.
The child that is not fed
He will not see,
Nor want to touch the flesh upon its bones - And still the fire burns.
The tiny grains of sand, particles of rock
That once stood proud over the crust
From whence it came
Is broken into what it used to be
And shifted by the tide of whim and give- to-me.
Tossed and eventually lost
On the angry sea of opportunity -
And still the fire burns.

Three Sons Of A Dead Man

You know, I was thinking last night
She said
As the tears rolled into her eyes,
How much like his father poor Georgy was
The night before he died.
And how much like Georgy your father is now.
That same air of ghostly pride.

Our once was man with a whip in his hand,
And the wheat slung over his shoulder.
Three bags he had carried at once in his day.
That once was droving man.

And now with eyes turned down
And colour grey
The wheat becomes his pillows
And the whip in his hand his life.

Tomorrow's Crim

Hey child, why do you cry?
And where is your mother son?
The light has long since left the school
And with it everyone.

With sad black eyes he looked at me
And said with hands on hips,
"My mother comes to get me soon.
She works just up the street.
She said that I must wait for her
Until she comes for me.

I had a key once 'round my neck
But then I lost it, see.
I gave it to the girl next door
So she would play with me."
Child. Why did your mother go?
"She has to work.
She told me so.
Our food and clothes and then the rent.
And daddy he spends every cent.

My daddy has a new car now
And mummy has a flat.
But gee it's cold. My shirt is old.
I put it on myself."

And then his pride had turned
To something less
As he put his tiny hands across his chest.
"Mummy goes to work before I wake.
She says 'we must get all that we can take.'

Shrew The Younger

Child you have a vicious tongue.
You've grown into a shrew.
You have the family wondering
What will become of you
We know you have a righteous streak
Anxiety drives the way you speak
But honestly child
Discover some mild
Your father couldn't sleep
Up half the night he walked the floor.
Just as well you closed your door
And into slumber deep.
He tossed the wrong inside his head
Problem sorted
Went to bed.
But laid there with his misery instead.
That tongue of yours,
That angry streak.
Tame it now.
It will make you weep.

The death Of Nanna

While asleep on the floor
At the foot of her bed
I heard an angel say
"Be quiet little spirit,
Don't make a sound.
I have come to take you away."

"No! No!" Cried the body
Imprisoning the soul
On her bed of torment lay.
"I don't know the place
Where you'll take me
And it's here I want to stay."

"Come home" said the angel.
"Just take my hand
And shake that shackle you wear.
That body is hardened
And wrinkled and cold
And you cannot stay in there."

Exhausted we slept till morning ray
Shone through the window to break the day.
But somewhere not to far from she
An angel waits on bended knee
To take a gentle spirit home to thee.
And when he does Lord
Comfort me.

The Fabric

In the early hours of Thursday
A vision came to me.
It was a piece of fabric
Torn for all the world to see.
The tear so wide and ugly
The cloth just wouldn't fit
In places where life's fabric
Was really meant to sit.

A voice within the stillness
Whispered "mend the fabric please"
It's soft and useless as it is
And given to disease.

Where do I start? I questioned.
My heart is not in this.
Mend the fabric came the answer.
Lest it rips beyond repair.

Just start above the damage
Where the fabric is still whole
Where the cloth is not corrupted
By the past.

If I muster up the spirit
And mend this gaping wound
Who's to say it will not split again
What good then is this pain?

I'd be safer- tell the stillness
If I simply never try
Or care about the fabric
Let it wither there and die.

Have courage. came the answer.
No time for your despair
A fabric is its strongest
At the mending of the tear.

Be Gone

You have to leave old man
He said.
We need to sell this place.
He said.
Pack up your belongs
And be gone.
The market is too good
To waste.
We'll get top price
If we make haste.
So pack up your belongs
And be gone.
Please let me stay.
I'm old and grey.
And son
You made a promise
to your mother.
You told her
You'd look after me.
But you are persuaded
By another.
To pack up my belongs
And be gone.
I have a garden.
Come and see.
It's here my friends
will come and visit me.
Can't you wait?

I'll soon be dead.
It's then
My son.
Your greedy self
Be fed.

Assaulted Housewife

That vacant stare says she's not there.
And hasn't been for years.
Her children crying on the street
Are lost amidst their fears.

Her eyes they have no light in them
As she looses courage to condemn
This one that's last of many men.

No need to carry bruises
To show that you're abused
The scars are real but hidden.
No love – No life - confused.

What can I say invisible one.
Rejected, worthless, beaten one.

The Rock Orchid

Faced with a question I had to ponder
My mind began to wander
When I came upon this orchid from the bush.
As I watched, my question floated
With its perfume
Then it halted
And it answered me as if I heard it speak.
"Just look at where I'm growing"
Says this plant with beauty glowing,
"This place is only for a chosen few.
It is possible," it told me,
"Come and sit a while and hold me.
Just look upon the poverty I have.
There is no soil to grow in
Where nourishment would flow in
And yet my blooms give joy to all who see.
Learn from me."
On this rock where life is hardest
Is the orchid at its best.
God gives us from the heart a simple quest.
Live poverty the hard and beauty blessed.

Wollongong

Between the cliffs of falling black rock
And the endless moving sea
There's a land just kissed by sunlight
And a breeze moves every tree.
Where gently falling raindrops
Joining heaven to our land
Bringing life unto our garden
Running streams and golden sand.

Where the might of man if present
In the cities overseen
By men hung under canvas
Spreading wings across the green.
While in the blue pacific
Giant ships from near and far
Are taking on their cargo
To make Australia what we are.

If you could sit on roof tops
You would hear in many tongues
The families 'round their tables
As they speak to little ones.
You would hear – if you would listen
Many different kinds of prayer.
In all the ways of praising God
For God is everywhere.

From its streets that teem with people
Along the arteries of roads
To the bushland and the farmland
Where a gentler life arose,
Then you would love this land we live in
South of Sydney, west of sea
Where the black rock's cut from sandstone
And the people here are free.

The Harvest

'Twas under the cover of night they came
To steal and crush the holy grape;
To vandalise the vineyard,
To spill the precious wine upon the barren soil.

With that stolen harvest and in the hour of darkness
The wine-press started its work:
It pressed from within –
Falling tears and sweat beaded on his emptiness.
As fear and indecision filled his heart,
He offered his spirit to the wine-press
In the lonely shadow – filled hours that followed.

It presses from without –
While the vandals judge the quality of the man.
They cannot see the beauty of the grape.
They have no light to fill their eyes.
Blindly they trick – interrogate.
Without appeal the fruit of the vine is silent and alone.

The vice begins its screwing down.
(for such is the work of the wine-press.)
The fruit was judged as poisonous and condemned.
They tied him to a whipping post –
To strip, to humiliate, to torture.
For such is the guilt of the wilful blind.

They crowned his head with thorns
And laid a cross upon his blood – soaked back
To drag through the streets to where he was to hang.
Through crowds that stood in silent watchful fear.
Through crowds that laughed and pushed and jeered.
Through crowds that cried their bitter helpless tears.
For the crowd who nailed him to the wood he cried.

The heavy body dragged against the nails that held him firm.
Between heaven and earth he hung till death confirmed.
With the wine-press pressing down against his breast
He surrenders his spirit to the keeper of the vineyard -
Who prepared for us the greatest vintage of all time.

Holy grape wrung out upon the wine-press of the cross
Stir our hearts to condemn the vandals of the vineyard,
To criticise the whims of the power – hungry blind,
Give us wine for our joy, strengthen our spirit.
Intoxicate us with your peace.

The Answer

When I was small
Not very tall.
The answer to life's questions
was the simplest quest of all.
To satisfy my worldly needs
I merely had to call.

I am hungry. Come and feed me.
I am thirsty. Need a drink.
If I was cold or wet or lonely
There was comfort
Didn't think.

When I was young
yet newly grown
and lacking the forbearance
to be shown

In fact I knew
the more I grew
the answer to life's questions (save a few)
I told the world how it should be.
To turn upon it's axis
just for me.

Now I am old
and not so bold.
The answer to life's questions hardly told.

There's a wisdom in not knowing
since the older that I'm growing,

That the questions without answers
create space.

Let the young ones have their certain
behind their theatre curtain
Leave me to sit and watch
with wrinkled face.

Hope

This will give hope
He pondered
At the ribboned gift he swore
"I'll bring it to her living space
and leave it at the door".

But as he sauntered up the path
Her door she opened wide
and begged the strangest messenger
to kindly come inside.

To her he presented a simple box
Wrapped and ribboned tenderly,
"'tis only small
cannot hold all
that you had hoped it be.

But this is all you've needed
to set your spirit free.
Gathered in this vessel
are the dreams you spoke to me.

she held it in her trembling hands
And speaking through her tears,
" Will that inside this ribboned box
give me back my years?"

Tell me, said the stranger
Your other hopes to be?
" Riches! Filled with riches
for my wealth and comfort be."
A fantasy.

Will it hold the latest medicines
to take away my ills?
Will it give me entertainment
and fill my days with thrills?

Historically though
There was a hope
I was pleased had come to naught.
Unanswered hopes will happen
for lessons soundly taught.

Trust me. This gift is only good
that I have brought to you
still sealed in darkness splendour
By a love that you once knew.

she spoke into the gift she held
This magic in my hand.
One hope I have above the rest
If life I could command:

A gift of hope to be understood
as I advance in years.
That intolerance of smarter minds
don't feed my growing fears.

I suggest you leave it lying
unopened on the shelf.
Ponder quietly at its contents
hoping varied kinds of wealth.

The lament of the constipated Dog

I needed to go
so I squatted outside
to poo as you do
But I couldn't abide
that long blades of grass
just painted my ass.

I can't go out here
It is perfectly clear
that my ass being tickled
just makes me feel queer.

So I left it
and left it
and left it some more
Till my person discovered
But she wasn't sure

How long it had been
since I pooed in the grass.
I wanted to tell her
" It tickled my ass."

A week and a day
had poolessly passed.
She became quite concerned
for the state of my ass.

My person, she took me
To visit the vet
who poked and then prodded

My pride was upset.

The vet told my person
that I'd have to stay
till I pooed with them watching.
I could just run away.

But she left me, my person.
With their eyes on my bum.
I cried in that place
for my person to come.

I just couldn't do
what they wanted me to
Not with them watching
my ass for a poo.

My person, she took me home
the next day.
The grass was cut short
in the yard where I play.

Don't look at me though
I hate being on show.
And an audience watching
just won't let me go.

Daddy Long Legs

Daddy was a spider
All legs and eyes
Daddy loved his dinner
Daddy dined on flies.

But Daddy was too greedy
as by and by you'll see.
He thought to catch a blow fly
But got instead a bee.

The bee looked at Daddy
And Daddy gave a spring.
He thought to catch a blow fly
But got instead a sting.

Poor Daddy long legs.
Sad sick and sore.
Never touch a blow fly.
no. never any more.

The hairy huntsman
laughed at him.
He couldn't catch a fly.
Confused and even frightened
He went quiet and shy.

He climbed into his hiding place.
To bind his wound and cry.

"How was that blow fly different?
I have to find out why.

I've always eaten blow fly
I do not understand.
I have to find out what went wrong.
I need to search the land.

If I could only see again
The blow fly with that sting
I know I'd be more careful
before I gave a spring."

So Daddy packed his spider web
and toothbrush in a swag
and set off to find this creature
In a passing shopping bag.

He climbed into the lady's bag
at the bus stop near his home
And rode with her all snug and quiet
As he began to roam.

In A Flash

Flick. .. And there it is
My memories and all
Mother peering down on me
From her portrait on the wall.

Aunty Esma's hanging next to her.
And there is uncle Fred.
I could swear that when I looked away
he slightly turned his head.

Eyes that tracked me from the frame
would speak if they had voice.
but alas she lost it years ago
in a coffin without choice.

A cockroach, startled hurried off
from his scavenge on a plate
to find himself a darker place
to hide away and wait.

The spider froze upon the frame
where in the dark his dinner came
and cursed the flash that
caused his meal to flee.

Esma smiled her worried smile
painted on for quite a while.

now mother cast her eyes
around to see.

The night outside is black and cold
in need of slumber deep
flicked off the light
in darkness safe returned to bed and sleep.

Monster

When I was only very small,
Not tall enough to reach the door
I used to sleep with Grandma down the hall.

To keep me tucked up nice and tight
Not game to move-
In rigid fright
There sits a monster under our bed
all night.

Dead still, except for trembling,
I'd strain my ears to hear
a slide, a growl of the monster near
somewhere under the bed.

" Listen! Listen!
Hear it tapping? Hear it scraping?
It's just waiting for your toes to touch the floor.
It would grab you before you ever reached the door.

I would have to reach up tall
to turn the latch.
But I'm too small
What can I do?
I need the loo!
Oh monster, go away I beg of you.

I can already feel
Its cold and slimy claws around my feet.
I dive deeper underneath
my grandma's sheet.

There I wait without a sound
'til sunrise spreads its light upon the ground.

Grandma says that monsters disappear
when daylight shines.
It slides into deep water
where it finds children playing
where they shouldn't be
Then it reaches up and drags them down for tea.

Sack him!

He called upon the Pope to sack the Bishop
because of what he knew and wouldn't tell.
Many people suffer from his silence.
Those who were abused have tasted hell.

But, Government, you live in a house of glass
and the queen should sack you too
you know about Nauru and Manus
and condoned the abuse they knew.

Now three long years the children suffer
locked for fear behind closed doors.
Secret walls surround the prison.
Freedom hopeless beyond its shores.

I call on Queen Elizabeth to sack the Liberal boss
Because of what he knows and will not tell
Many people suffer from his silence.
Those who are abused are tasting hell.

Storm At Sea

I was standing by the ocean watching
waves upon the beaches breaking.
Pondering the violent notion
Of the waves at sea.

I mused about the storm that passes
rising far from where this place is
sending troubled seas
along my way.

Deep within the ocean stirring
came a voice for my occurring;
Without the storm,
in stagnant stillness,
lacking movement
Nothing grows.

There Is Still Time

I fought with you one yesterday
And caused that you should have to go away.
Too painful for us both if you would stay.

In the time we knew
A chasm grew
Never more our friendship would be true.

I've relived the conversation
and the words that's left unsaid
as they break into my dreaming
where I toss and turn in bed.

" If I'd have said it this way
Your reply might have been that
Heartbreak would have been averted
Through the courage of our diplomat.

Waking from my slumber this grey morn
I missed the friendship we so carelessly had torn
And so to self reflectively I scorn.

Many wounded yesterdays have passed
now the hidden unforgiven must not last.
The dye of never mending is not cast.

There is still time for rifts to mend
I fear not much before my journey's end.
Giving voice to words unspoken now depend
on a humble willingness for one to bend.

Our peace I fear cannot be truly made
Once our bodies are both buried and decayed.
Tomb stones cold cannot offer joy
Silence now forever love destroy.

Waiting for the train

Waiting is an empty space
that's filled with dreams and lists to make
Of something that I have to do
and things that I have missed to take.

While waiting for my train I note
That woman over there
Has her pants just way too tight.
Uncomfortable to wear?
Her belly hanging over-belt
with nowhere else to go
Her top rides up above the bulge
has nakedness on show.

I must not stare
I'll look elsewhere
and resume my idle thoughts
where waiting makes an empty space
and daydream has its sport.

Across the track in front of me
is everyone that I can see
just looking at a phone.
Lost to them the art of dreaming.
In their hand dictates are screaming
Never be alone.

There's a man in a wheelchair
not far from me.
He has no legs that I can see.
In the space where his legs should be
his shopping sits quite comfortably.
Good use he's made of the space provided
for shopping bags and things decided
to take them home for tea.

A judgement I have made on one
While waiting for my train to come .
That jeans with cuts where knees hang out
are not for winter winds about.

Silly girl with hands on knees
to protect them from the chilly breeze
should consider body needs
Less what the world of fashion sees.

Now, where was I?
Oh yes I know
There was that place I'd like to go?
Where colours are the best on show
for trees and blooms on plants that grow.

Rushing water in a mountain stream
that talks to pebbles washing clean.
And grasses after summer rain
That smell so sweet ……
Oh here's my train.

When The Bottle Is Empty

When the bottle is empty
and the children have fled
Where now is the drunkard
to lay down his head?

He searches the bar- room
for someone to follow
to give him some money
for more grog to swallow

He staggers and stumbles.
His dignity torn.
Others stare with detachment
A friendship has gone.

So what can be done
with the drunk on the stool?
His wives and his children
see a dangerous fool.

"Pity me now,"
Says the face full of sorrow
abandoned and loveless
He alone makes tomorrow.

The Zippi-Uppi-Thing

The answer to life's questions
All we have of any worth
is the zippi-uppi thing
It hides the future of the earth.

It comes in many lengths and strengths
and answers to my call.
The zippi-uppi thing is blind
Unattended it will fall.

Take warning though my travellers
That the pain won't go away
from unrestrained and careless use
of the zippi-uppi thing at play.

So if you've overstayed your welcome
said things you can't retrieve
use your zippi-uppi thing
and quietly take your leave.

Never underestimate
the zippi-uppi thing
It's origin is wisdom
It's deliverance a sting.

For The Love Of Little Things

For the love of little things
For things that crawl
with tiny wings
Where honey bee and blowfly sing

I grew a flower garden
outside the window, by my chair
so I could watch them working
and listen to their prayer.

Tiny creatures, 'oft unnoticed
Singing songs so soft and clear.
Useful creatures, 'oft unnoticed
changing worlds both far and near.

For the love of little things
I ponder life with little wings
They feed the world with what they do.
And take away our rubbish too.

Pollinating fruits and flowers
eating bodies dead for hours
Without such work 'be body towers.
Reaching for the moon.

There are some creatures we will find.
(though very few to keep in mind)
As with humans are inclined
to sting and bite 'oft out of sight.

Bugs we assault with slap and squeeze
And tell the God we are displeased
with a creation such as these.
And demand that it should stop.

A timely word to human kind
Our little ones are in decline
stop killing off our bugs to feed your greed
For once they go this world will know
that absolutely nothing more will grow.

But of the many thousand things
That creep and crawl with tiny wings
I love bees most of all.

Let's Be Honest

It has come to my attention
so it's really worth a mention
that the process we call honesty
is disappearing into mist.

The lies I've had to swallow
In my spirit leaves a hollow
have been mounting ever rapidly since youth.
If you want me to believe you tell the truth.

The old folks had a saying
in our history long since playing
From a thief you have protection that will last.
Simply lock the goods you value
in a secure place you come to
and you will have your things when thief has passed.

Of the liar we are fearful
No security is mindful
With the stealing of our dignity we fall.

The liar takes our foolishness
and that becomes the tool
to manipulate our trustfulness
to crush the ancient rule.

Sure. Storytellers have their craft
that lead us on a vision path
of fear intrigue or laughter
stimulating reason ever after.

But if you want me to believe you tell the truth.

" It will be done" the Pollies say.
" But it hasn't been done yet.
And that was simply years ago
You thought we would forget.

They tell us what we want to hear
It's in the wind: election's near.
" I'll get it done once I have won
We've heard it all before.
If you want me to believe you tell the truth.

Questions

Unanswered, unimagined , unwanted.
Are questions she would rather were not asked
Questions a response would not hold fast.
Honesty a thing of childhood past.

Ask the question of the woman caught in fear
and all you'll get is what she wants to hear.
A lie.
Because the truth is much too painful in reply.

'How are you feeling, woman?
Are you peaceful?
Are you well? '

'The answer to your query
I'm afraid I cannot tell. '
Honesty won't profit
In the woman's house of Hell.

' And your children: are they with you?
Are they clothed
and are they fed?
Or did somebody take them
to a safer place instead?

Tormented stare
Response beguiled.
Hell is not a fitting place
To house a frightened child.

The Spider

I had a conversation
with the spider on my mirror.
He was fighting his reflection
and intending upon war.

The image he was fighting
was an image of himself
The unforgiving; that reflects
The image of himself.

His enemy moved when spider did
seemly knowing his intent
The image froze when spider did
and shadowed where he went.

Next morning, in the bathroom
I viewed a tragic show
The spider weak and dying
never willing to let go.

"Give up, little spider
You're dying hanging there
It won't give up 'till you do
Now it's clinging to despair."

The Author

www.ingramcontent.com/pod-product-compliance
Ingram Content Group UK Ltd.
Pitfield, Milton Keynes, MK11 3LW, UK
UKHW022220230426
12048UKWH00016BA/961